Christmas 1994

To: Sheryl Fulcher

From: Emmanuel Reformed Church
Grade 1 & 2 Sunday School
Class

Teachers: Yvonne Post
&
Jacqueline Verhoog

NOTE TO PARENTS

This familiar Bible story has been retold in a sensitive and simple way so that young children can read and understand it for themselves. But the special message of the story remains unchanged. It is the message of God's love and care for us all.

Published in Great Britain by World International Publishing Ltd.
Published in the United States by Tyndale House Publishers, Inc.,
Wheaton, Illinois.
Printed in Germany.
ISBN 08423-1301-7
01 00 99 98 97 96 95 94
9 8 7 6 5 4 3 2 1

A Very Special Baby

Retold by Kenneth N. Taylor
Illustrated by Edgar Hodges

Tyndale House Publishers, Inc.,
Wheaton, Illinois.

Long ago, in the city of Nazareth, God sent an angel down from heaven to tell a young woman named Mary something very wonderful.

The angel told Mary she would have a baby!
"Name him Jesus," said the angel. "He will
be God's Son."

This man is Joseph. He is a good man, and he and Mary will soon get married.

Mary is telling him what the angel said. Do you remember what it was? That she would have a baby named Jesus, and God would be his Father.

Mary and Joseph had to take a long trip to the town of Bethlehem. In those days long ago there were no cars, so they had to walk. Mary rode the donkey because she was tired. It was almost time for her to have her baby, God's Son.

When they got to Bethlehem, all the places to stay were full. The man is telling them that he has no more rooms, but they can sleep in the barn with the cows and donkeys.

That night Mary had her baby. They wrapped him in soft strips of cloth and laid him in a bed of hay. Mary and Joseph named the baby Jesus, just as the angel had said.

That night some shepherds were watching their sheep. Suddenly, an angel was standing there beside them. The shepherds were very frightened at first. But the angel said, "Don't be afraid. I have wonderful news for you. Tonight God's Son has been born."

Suddenly there was a bright light in the sky.
The shepherds looked up and saw hundreds of
angels. The angels were very happy and sang,
"Glory to God in heaven, and peace on earth
for all those pleasing him."

The shepherds jumped up and said to each other, "Let's go and see this baby who will become our Savior." They hurried along the road to Bethlehem and found the baby lying in a manger, just as the angels had said. They got on their knees and worshiped the baby because he was their King.

One day some wise men from a country far away came to worship Jesus. Can you see them on their camels?

They had seen a bright star and knew this meant that God's Son would be born. So they had come to worship him.

They went to the king's palace because they thought that the King of God's people would be born there.

But no one at the palace had heard about Jesus. And King Herod was afraid this new King might take his place.

Then the wise men saw the star again, and it led them to Bethlehem.

They found the house where Mary and
Joseph and the baby Jesus had moved.

When they walked inside, they worshiped Jesus and gave him gifts — gold, frankincense, and myrrh. These are the kind of gifts people give to kings. They knew that Jesus was going to be a great King.

Soon afterwards God sent a dream to Joseph. "You must take Mary and the baby and escape to the country of Egypt," God said, "for King Herod wants to kill Jesus." Joseph took Mary and Jesus and escaped to Egypt safely.

When it was safe to go home, God told Mary and Joseph they could return to Nazareth. There, Jesus grew up and did many wonderful things to show people God's love.

Jesus was a very special baby!

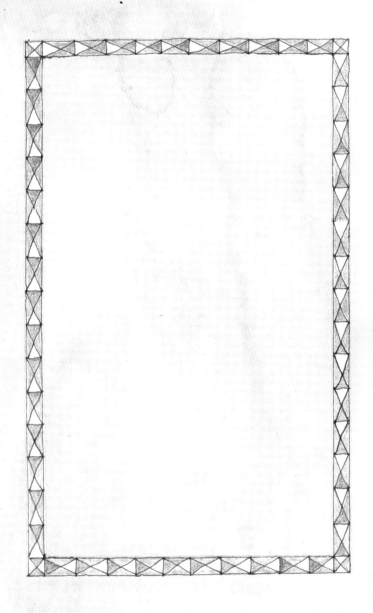